Sam in the Cab

By Debbie Croft

Bec can see Sam.

Sam is in the cab.

Sam sits in the cab.

Sam can ram at the pit.

Ram ... ram ... ram!

Bam!

Sam rams a tap!

The cab has hit the tap!

Bec has a hat.

It fits the tap.

Sam can see the hat!

CHECKING FOR MEANING

1. What did Sam hit when he was digging? *(Literal)*

2. Who has a hat that fits the tap? *(Literal)*

3. Why did Sam hit the tap with the cab? *(Inferential)*

EXTENDING VOCABULARY

ram	Look at the word *ram*. Can you think of other words that rhyme with *ram*?
Bam	Look at the word *Bam*. Ask, what does the word *Bam* mean? What other words could you use?
fits	Look at the word *fits*. How many sounds are in this word? What are they?

MOVING BEYOND THE TEXT

1. How do you think Sam felt when he hit the tap at the pit? Why?

2. Have you ever accidentally knocked something over? How did you feel?

3. What do you think might happen next in the story? Why?

SPEED SOUNDS

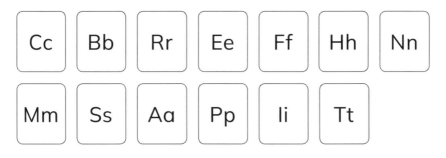

Cc	Bb	Rr	Ee	Ff	Hh	Nn
Mm	Ss	Aa	Pp	Ii	Tt	

PRACTICE WORDS

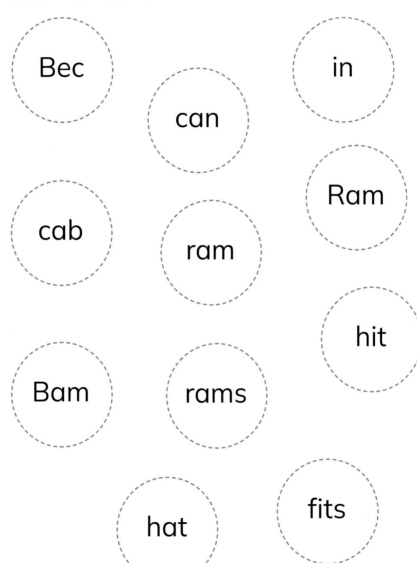

Bec

in

can

cab

Ram

ram

hit

Bam

rams

hat

fits